Body Talk

Pump It Up
RESPIRATION AND CIRCULATION

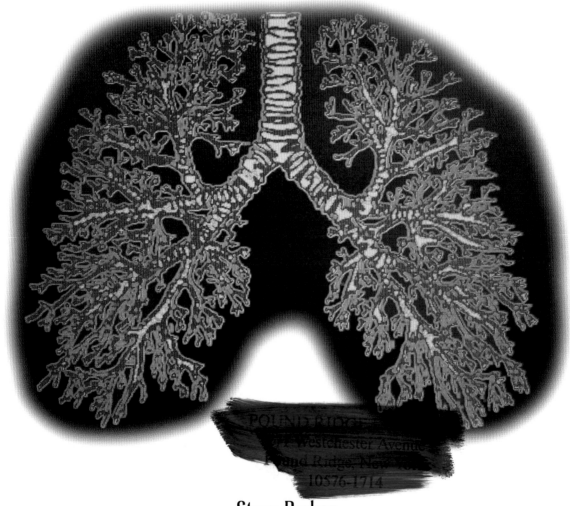

Steve Parker

Raintree
Chicago, Illinois

For information, address the publisher
Raintree, 100 N. LaSalle, Suite 1200
Chicago, IL 60602
Customer Service 888-363-4266
Visit our website at www.raintreelibrary.com

Printed and bound in China, by South China Printing Company Ltd

10 09 08 07 06
10 9 8 7 6 5 4 3 2 1

Library of Congress Cataloging-in-Publication Data
Parker, Steve.
    Pump it up! : respiration and circulation / Steve Parker.
        p. cm. -- (Body talk)
    Includes index.
    ISBN 1-4109-1878-5 (lib. bdg.) -- ISBN 1-4109-1885-8 (pbk.)
    1. Respiration--Juvenile literature. 2. Blood--Circulation--Juvenile literature. I. Title. II. Series: Parker, Steve. Body talk.
    QP121.P276 2006
    612.1--dc22
                                        2005027518

Acknowledgments
The publishers would like to thank the following for permission to reproduce photographs:
Alamy Images p. 35 (ImageState), p. 18-19 (Redferns Music Picture Library); Corbis pp. 4-5, 7, 16-17, 22-23, 39; 30-31 (Annie Griffiths Belt), p. 12 (Christian Liewig), pp. 26-27 (Don Mason), p. 28 (Lester Lefkowitz), pp. 36-37 (Michael & Patricia Fogden), p. 9 (Reuters), p. 14 (Saba/Marc Asnin), pp. 40-41 (Stephanie Maze); Getty pp. 20, 32-33; 21 (Digital Vision), pp. 37, 40 (PhotoDisc), p. 8 (Stone); Harcourt Education Ltd/Tudor Photography pp. 6-7; Richard Smith p. 41; Science Photo Library pp. 28-29; pp. 10-11 (Alfred Pasieka), pp. 38-39 (Andrew Syred); pp. 23, 24-25, 42-43 (BSIP), p. 25 (CNRI), p. 18 (David M Martin, MD), pp. 12-13, 42-43 (Eye of Science), pp. 42-43 (Herve Conge, ISM), p. 10 (J. L. Carson, Custom Medical Stock, Photo), p. 31 (Mark Thomas), p. 26 (Saturn Stills), p. 11 (Simon Fraser), p. 9 (Steve Vowles), pp. 34-35 (Susumu Nishinaga), pp. 14-15 (Tony McConnell). Cover photograph reproduced with permission of Getty Images/ Reportage / Daniel Berehulak.
Artwork by Darren Linguard and Jeff Edwards.

Every effort has been made to contact copyright holders of any material reproduced in this book. Any omissions will be rectified in subsequent printings if notice is given to the publishers.

The paper used to print this book comes from sustainable resources.

Disclaimer
All the Internet addresses (URLs) given in this book were valid at the time of going to press. However, due to the dynamic nature of the Internet, some addresses may have changed, or sites may have ceased to exist since publication. While the author and publishers regret any inconvenience this may cause readers, no responsibility for any such changes can be accepted by either the author or the publishers.

Dedicated to the memory of Lucy Owen

Contents

Any words appearing in the text in bold, **like this,** are explained in the glossary. You can also look out for them in "Body language" at the bottom of each page.

Breathe and Beat

When was the last time you got out of breath? Not just puffing, but really gasping? Maybe it was after an important race or during some exciting sport. Perhaps you were running for the last bus or train, or rushing to see the latest movie.

Bursting lungs, pounding heart

When you are really out of breath, your only thought is to get more air. Did you feel, as some people say, that your lungs might burst? Did you also feel your heart pounding and thumping? It might have even seemed ready to leap out of your chest.

When the body is active, breathing speeds up and the heart races. It is the body's way of taking in more oxygen, which we can't live without. Afterwards, we may flop down totally exhausted.

organ   major part of the body, such as the brain, liver, or heart

Nonstop actions

But soon, after a short rest, you get back to normal. Then you hardly notice your breathing and your heartbeat. Yet they go on every second, all day and night, for a whole lifetime.

Breathing and heartbeat rely on three **organs** that are vital for life. Two of these are your lungs, which take in air. Your lungs take **oxygen** from air and help get it into your blood. The third is your heart, which pumps your blood all around your body to deliver the oxygen where it is needed. So breathing and beating must never stop. Otherwise, life does too.

Find out later

Why do we need sticky mucus?

How does breathing change your voice?

Why go batty about blood?

oxygen gas which makes up one-fifth of air, and which the body needs

Must Have Air!

Breathing equipment

Air comes into the body through the nose, down through the throat and trachea, to tubes in the chest called **bronchi**. These carry the air to the two lungs. Together with the heart, the lungs fill most of the chest.

The must-have substance that your body needs to stay alive is all around you. You can't see it, smell it, or taste it, but it is vital for life. It is air.

The air is a mixture of gases. You breathe all of these gases in and out. But your body needs only one of them, **oxygen.** Oxygen makes up about one-fifth of the air. The other gases are nitrogen, **carbon dioxide,** and water vapor, which pass harmlessly in and out of our bodies.

We cannot see the air we ➤ breathe as it goes in and out of our lungs. But we know it is there, since it can fill a balloon.

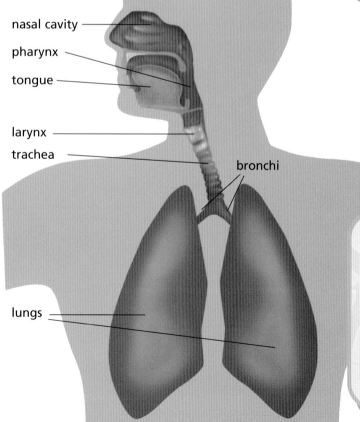

nasal cavity

pharynx

tongue

larynx

trachea

bronchi

lungs

DID YOU KNOW?

Free diving is a very special sport where people hold their breath for several minutes as they go very deep underwater. Free divers train for years, have many fitness checks, and always have a medical expert on hand when they attempt a dive. Can you find out the world record for free diving?

bronchi   large air tubes that branch from the bottom of the trachea and carry air into the lungs
carbon dioxide   waste gas made by the body and breathed out

The breathing system

A whole set of parts inside your body is designed to take the oxygen from the air around you to the blood inside of you. It also gets rid of the waste gas carbon dioxide that your body produces as it works.

This set of parts is called the **respiratory system.** The parts work together to take in fresh air, get some oxygen from it, pass this oxygen to the blood, push out the waste carbon dioxide, and prepare to take in fresh air again.

The need to breathe

The body's need to get oxygen and to get rid of waste carbon dioxide is so great that we always have to breathe. Some people can hold their breath underwater for a long time. But they soon feel a great urge to breathe again, so they must come back to the surface.

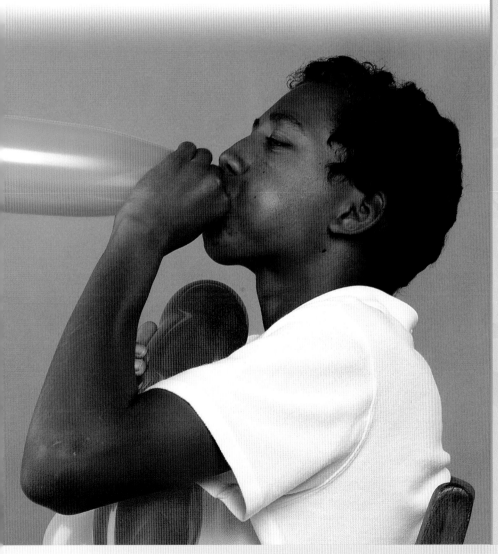

respiratory system   nose, mouth, pharynx, larynx, trachea, bronchi, lungs

Sticky and slimy

The inside of your nose makes a cupful of sticky mucus each day to catch dirt and germs. As the mucus collects this material, it slides into the throat for swallowing. Dusty or smoky air makes the nose produce much more mucus. So do certain illnesses, such as the common cold.

Sniff, sniff

Do you always breathe through your nose? If you have a cold, you may have to breathe through your mouth. But the nose has small hairs in its two nostrils to trap bits of floating dust and dirt and make the air cleaner as it gets to the lungs. Inside, the nose has a sticky lining of slimy **mucus** to trap more dust and germs.

Built-in air machine

The mucus lining inside your nose is moist or damp and gives off moisture to the air as it passes through. This makes sure that the air does not dry out your lungs when it gets there. Inside your nose there are also a lot of very small **blood vessels** just under the surface. The warm blood in these vessels warms up the cold air. So your nose is your built-in air machine that makes air clean, warm, and moist, just how your lungs like it.

Top athletes breathe hard ➤ and fast to get every bit of air into their lungs. Some wear sticky patches on their noses, to help keep the airways as wide open as possible.

◄ A sneeze blasts millions of tiny drops of mucus into the air. It is best to catch them in a tissue or handkerchief, so other people do not breathe them, especially when you have a cold.

blood vessels   arteries, capillaries, and veins through which blood flows

Air, food, air, food

The back of your nose leads to your throat and so does the back of your mouth. The throat is a tube for both air and food. At the bottom it splits into two tubes. One is the trachea to your lungs. The other, the esophagus, goes to your stomach.

If you mix breathing and swallowing, it can be very serious. If you try to eat and swallow while talking or running, a lump of food could go down the wrong way. This could block your trachea and cause choking, which can kill you.

Bleeding nose

The small blood vessels inside the nose are delicate. A bump can easily break them and cause a nosebleed. The usual treatment is to pinch the nose shut for several minutes until the bleeding stops.

mucus   sticky fluid in various body parts that helps gather dust and germs and helps substances move easily

Down, down, down

Air going into the body is similar to you going into a deep underground cave or mine. It soon becomes very dark, and there are passages on either side. This happens as air goes down your throat and trachea, into your chest. At the bottom, the trachea branches into two slightly narrower tubes, called **bronchi**. One of these leads to the left lung, the other to the right.

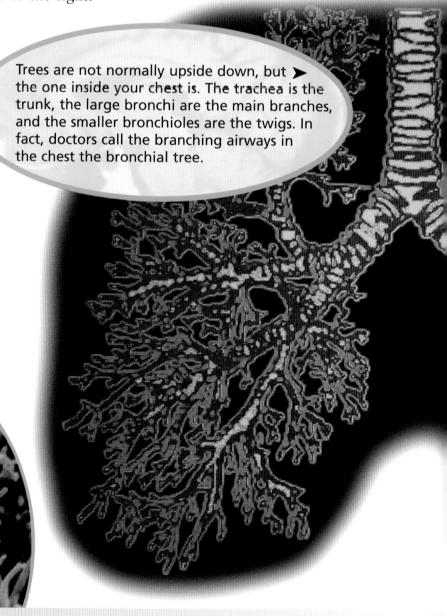

Trees are not normally upside down, but ➤ the one inside your chest is. The trachea is the trunk, the large bronchi are the main branches, and the smaller bronchioles are the twigs. In fact, doctors call the branching airways in the chest the bronchial tree.

Clearing your throat

The main air tubes are lined with sticky **mucus** to trap dirt and germs. The lining also has millions of tiny hairs, called **cilia**. These wave to make the mucus move slowly upwards, to the top of the trachea. Now and then we cough it up and swallow it, which is called clearing your throat.

cilia

mucus

cartilage   tough, springy substance that forms some parts of the skeleton

Thinner, shorter

Slightly farther along, each of the bronchi splits into two more smaller tubes. This happens again and again, about 15 times. The air tubes get even thinner and shorter, and are called **bronchioles.** Finally the air is deep inside the lungs, ready to give up its oxygen.

Open under pressure

Inside the body, parts of the respiratory system are squeezed together under pressure. If the windpipe, bronchi, and other air tubes were not supported, they would be squashed flat. So they have hooplike shapes of a stiff substance called **cartilage.** These cartilage rings keep the airways open, but are able to bend easily. If your windpipe could not bend, you would have a very stiff neck!

Don't clog up

A river stops flowing if it gets clogged up with mud, rocks, and tree limbs. Smoking tobacco can clog up the lungs. The smoke kills the tiny cilia hairs that keep mucus flowing up and out of the lungs. Then the mucus, with trapped dirt and germs, collects in your lungs and can cause disease.

cilia microscopic hairs on the cells in various body parts that wave back and forth

Millions of Bubbles

Plenty of room

The lung's air bubbles, alveoli, can be seen only under a microscope. There are over 400 million in both lungs. If they were all joined together and ironed flat, they would cover a whole tennis court. This is enough surface area for the body to get all the oxygen it needs.

As air reaches the deepest, darkest parts of your lungs, it is halfway through its journey. It flows into millions of tiny caves, each one far too small to see. These caves are like air bubbles and are called **alveoli.** They make the lungs feel like a sponge. Around each one is a net of even tiny blood vessels, called **capillaries.** At last, this is where the body will get its **oxygen.**

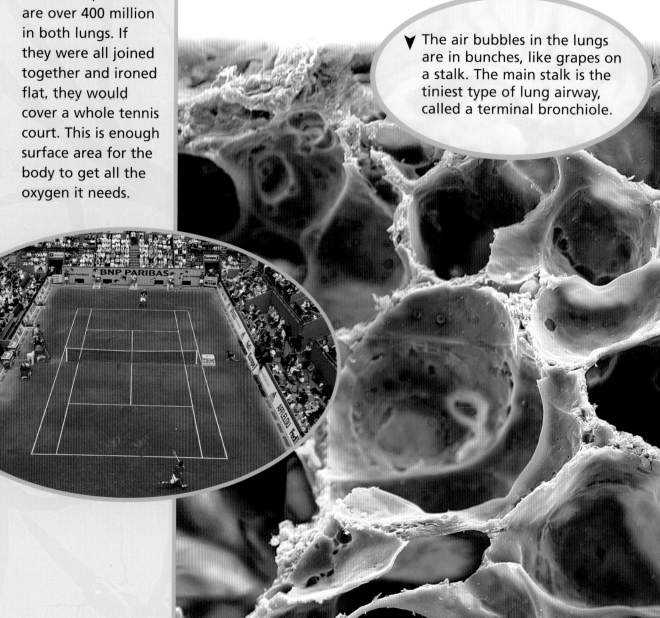

▼ The air bubbles in the lungs are in bunches, like grapes on a stalk. The main stalk is the tiniest type of lung airway, called a terminal bronchiole.

alveoli　tiny air spaces in the lungs, where oxygen is passed into blood vessels and carbon dioxide is taken out

Oxygen in

The walls of the alveoli and capillaries are incredibly thin. Oxygen easily passes from the air-filled alveoli through to the blood in the capillaries. This happens in millions of alveoli and capillaries all through the lungs. In just a second or two, the body has enough oxygen from the fresh, breathed-in air. The capillaries carry the blood and oxygen to larger blood vessels, which move the blood throughout the body.

bronchiole

Another smoking disease

Smoking tobacco does not only cause infections and cancers in the lungs. It also causes emphysema. The tiny air bubbles become flattened out and joined. This means there is less surface area for taking in oxygen, and people get out of breath.

DOWN THE AIRWAYS

Trachea (including larynx)	6 in (15 cm) long
Main bronchi	Left 2 in (5 cm) long Right 1.2 in (3 cm) long
Medium bronchi	0.4–0.8 in (1-2 cm) long
Small bronchi	0.08–0.2 in (1-5 mm) long
Smallest bronchi (bronchioles)	0.04–0.08 in (up to 1mm) long
Alveoli	0.01 in (0.25 mm) across

capillaries tiniest blood vessels with very thin walls that let oxygen, nutrients, and waste pass between the blood and cells

Straight trade

The amount of air you breathe out is about the same as you breathe in. Yet your body has used up some **oxygen** from breathed-in air. So what is added to breathed-out air? The answer is another gas, **carbon dioxide,** which is one of the body's natural waste products.

Asthma

The condition called **asthma** makes breathing difficult. It happens when the lining of the small airway in the lungs swells up, making the breathing tubes narrow. Asthma can be triggered by exercise, cold air or **allergies** to dust and other substances. Treatment is usually a medical drug in the form of a breathed-in spray, (below) that opens up the tubes again.

▲ Some illnesses affect the body's ability to take in oxygen, so the person breathes pure oxygen through a mask.

diffusion   movement of a substance from a place where there is a lot of it to a place where there is less of it so the substance is evenly spread out

One in, one out

Blood collects carbon dioxide from all around the body. As blood flows to the capillaries in the lungs, it contains a lot of it. In the lungs, as oxygen is passed into the blood, the alveoli take carbon dioxide out of the blood. Oxygen and carbon dioxide trade places, moving from areas where there are high levels, to areas that have less. This spreading out is called **diffusion.**

Back again

Almost as soon as you take air into your lungs, you are ready to blow it out again. The air is now stale, with less oxygen but more carbon dioxide. It flows back along the bronchiole tubes, into the bronchi, up the trachea, and finally out. The whole journey lasts three or four seconds and then begins all over again with fresh air.

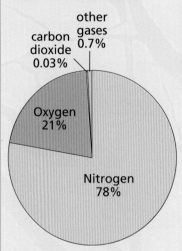

Air breathed in

other gases 0.7%
carbon dioxide 0.03%
Oxygen 21%
Nitrogen 78%

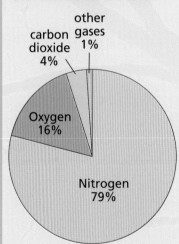

Air breathed out

other gases 1%
carbon dioxide 4%
Oxygen 16%
Nitrogen 79%

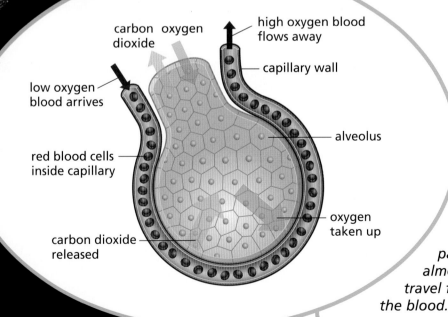

carbon dioxide
oxygen
high oxygen blood flows away
capillary wall
low oxygen blood arrives
red blood cells inside capillary
alveolus
carbon dioxide released
oxygen taken up

The walls of the alveoli and capillary added together are probably a thousand times thinner than this page. Oxygen has almost no distance to travel from the air to the blood.

Breathing and Talking

What do you do 30,000 times every day, almost without realizing? Breathe! When you're sitting relaxed or are asleep, you breathe in and then out every three or four seconds. Breathing gets faster, once every second, when you are active and your muscles need more oxygen.

Muscle power

All body movements, including breathing, are powered by muscles. Breathing uses two main sets of muscles.

The first is a sheet of muscle that looks like an upside down bowl under your lungs. It is called the **diaphragm.** As it **contracts,** it becomes flatter. This stretches the lungs down and as they get bigger, air moves in to fill the space.

Breathing uses two main sets of muscles below the lungs and between the ribs.

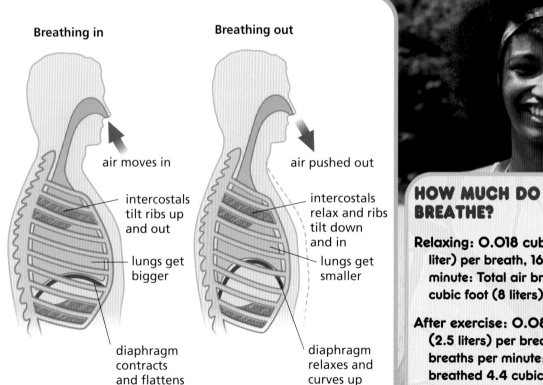

Breathing in

air moves in

intercostals tilt ribs up and out

lungs get bigger

diaphragm contracts and flattens

Breathing out

air pushed out

intercostals relax and ribs tilt down and in

lungs get smaller

diaphragm relaxes and curves up

HOW MUCH DO YOU BREATHE?

Relaxing: 0.018 cubic foot (0.5 liter) per breath, 16 breaths per minute: Total air breathed 0.28 cubic foot (8 liters) per minute.

After exercise: 0.088 cubic foot (2.5 liters) per breath, 50 breaths per minute: Total air breathed 4.4 cubic foot (125 liters) per minute

abdomen   lower part of the body or torso

The second set are long, narrow muscles between each pair of your ribs. They are called **intercostals** and as they contract, they move the ribs up and out. This stretches the lungs forwards, again making them bigger so air moves in.

Out again

To breathe out, the diaphragm and intercostals relax. The lungs have been stretched like a blown up balloon, and now spring back to their smaller size, pushing out air. The whole process is controlled by your brain. This is an automatic process which works on its own, so you don't have to worry about it.

Brain in control

Your brain has tiny sensors that detect the amounts of oxygen and carbon dioxide in the blood flowing through it. If there is too much carbon dioxide and too little oxygen, control centers in the brain (see below) send nerve messages to the breathing muscles, telling them to work harder and faster.

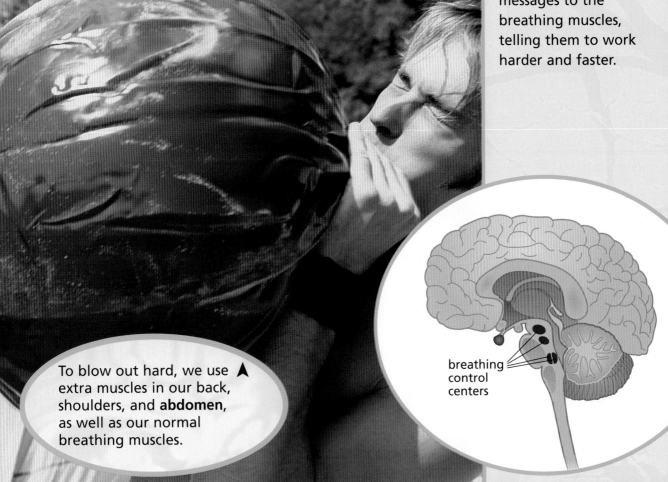

To blow out hard, we use ▲ extra muscles in our back, shoulders, and **abdomen**, as well as our normal breathing muscles.

breathing control centers

contract become smaller or shorter, as when a muscle contracts and pulls on the bones attached to it

Vocal cords

In quiet breathing, the vocal cords are apart, with a gap between called the **glottis** (below). Air goes past easily and silently. In speech, larynx muscles pull the cords so they almost touch.

vocal cord

"Hello, how are you?"

How many times have you spoken today? Imagine life if no one could talk. We not only talk, we also make other noises, such as laughter, shouts, and maybe even crying. These sounds are made because of the **respiratory system.** The sounds come from your **larynx,** also called your voicebox. This is inside your neck.

Box of tricks

Your larynx is made of curved pieces of strong **cartilage** and muscles that move them. Inside it has two narrow flaps, one sticking out from either side, called **vocal cords.** When you breathe normally, the air passes through a triangle-shaped gap between the vocal cords.

If you want to speak, muscles pull the vocal cords almost together. As air passes through the very narrow gap between them, it makes the cords **vibrate** very quickly. This causes the sound of your voice.

Shaping the sounds

The sounds from your vocal cords are fairly quiet. They are made louder, into clearly spoken words, by the air passages of your throat and mouth, your tongue and lips, and by the air space inside your nose. Pinch your nose shut and talk, and you soon hear how much your nose adds to your voice!

Out, out, out
The voicebox is designed to work with breathed-out air. Try to speak while breathing in, and see how difficult it is. Also the air flows very slowly when you talk. Read out loud and time how long you keep going before you need to breathe in. Compare this with the time for breathing out and then in normally.

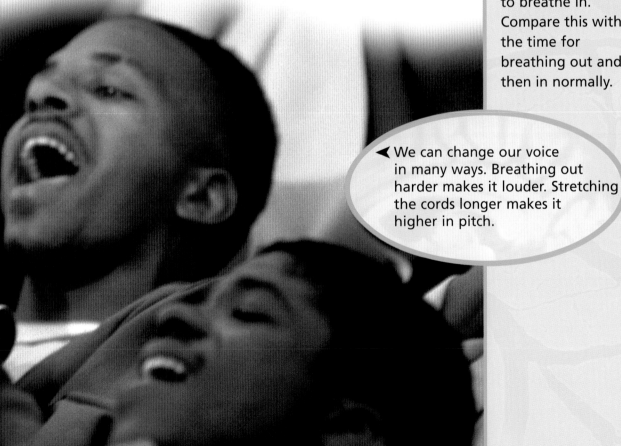

◄ We can change our voice in many ways. Breathing out harder makes it louder. Stretching the cords longer makes it higher in pitch.

Hardworking Heart

If there was an award for the hardest working part of the body, it would surely go to the heart. Every second, night and day, year after year, your heart thumps and pounds and squeezes and pumps. It sends blood on its never ending journey around and around your body.

Your blood carries **oxygen** from your lungs, as well as **nutrients** from food and hundreds of other substances, to every part of you.

Heart ache, heart break

We often speak of the heart when talking about strong feelings and emotions. These feelings are not in the heart, they are in the brain. But the brain does make the heart beat faster when we are very excited, sad, or stressed in some way.

Where is the heart?

The heart is perhaps smaller than many people think. Your heart is about the size of your clenched fist. It is also lower and more central in the body than people imagine. It lies behind the lower breastbone, with its lower end just to the left side. It is surrounded by the two lungs. The left lung has a scooped-out shape where most of the heart fits. This makes the left lung smaller than the right lung.

nutrients substances in food that the body needs to grow, be healthy, and heal from injuries

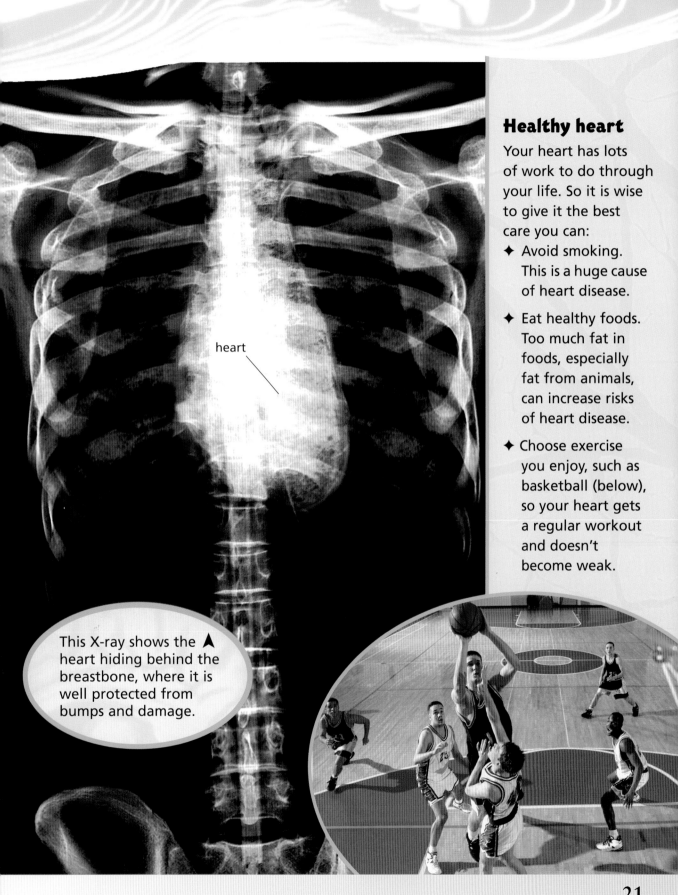

heart

This X-ray shows the ▲ heart hiding behind the breastbone, where it is well protected from bumps and damage.

Healthy heart

Your heart has lots of work to do through your life. So it is wise to give it the best care you can:

✦ Avoid smoking. This is a huge cause of heart disease.

✦ Eat healthy foods. Too much fat in foods, especially fat from animals, can increase risks of heart disease.

✦ Choose exercise you enjoy, such as basketball (below), so your heart gets a regular workout and doesn't become weak.

Two hearts in one

Do you have two hearts? Not quite. But your heart is not just one pump. It is two pumps, side by side. This is because your body has two routes for blood, known as circulations. One circulation is quite short. It is the **pulmonary circulation** from the heart to the lungs, then back again. Blood flowing around this circulation gathers oxygen from the lungs and comes back refreshed and bright red.

There and back, twice

When oxygen-filled blood returns from the lungs to the heart, it sets off on the second blood route, the **systemic circulation**, which is much longer. This takes the blood all around the body to deliver its oxygen, nutrients, and other substances. As the blood gives up oxygen, its color changes from bright red to reddish-blue.

Two pumps, two routes

The body's two circulations form a figure-8, with the heart at the crossover. The left side of the heart has thicker walls and is more powerful than the right side, because the systemic route all around the body is much longer than the pulmonary route to the lungs.

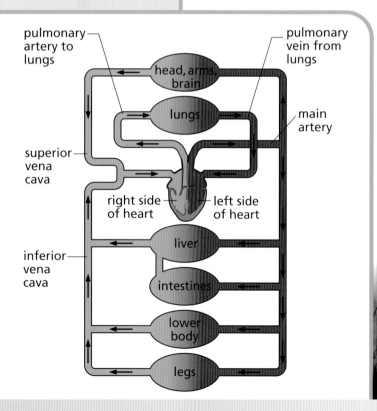

pulmonary artery to lungs

pulmonary vein from lungs

head, arms, brain

lungs

main artery

superior vena cava

right side of heart

left side of heart

inferior vena cava

liver

intestines

lower body

legs

We make many kinds ➤ of pumping machines for liquids, such as this oil pump, or nodding donkey. Most last 10 years, maybe 20 at the most. Yet some hearts keep pumping for over 100 years!

Left and right

Why doesn't blood on the two routes get mixed up in the heart? Because the heart is two separate pumps. Blood from the right pump goes to the lungs. It comes back to the left pump. This sends the blood all around the body. Then it comes back to the right pump to get more oxygen, and the journey begins again.

Nonstop muscle

The walls of the heart (above) are a special kind of muscle called **cardiac** muscle or **myocardium**. This keeps working without getting tired. Plenty of exercise and activity makes the heart beat harder and faster, keeping the muscle thick and strong.

myocardium   muscle in the walls of the heart

A heartbeat away

Your heart is not only your body's hardest-working part, it is also the noisiest! You can't hear your own heart because your ears are too far away. But listening to someone else's heart, by pressing an ear to the chest, reveals its steady beat: lub-dup, lub-dup, lub-dup.

This is not the sound of the heart muscle pumping. It is the noise made by parts inside called **valves,** as they snap shut with each beat. The valves make sure blood keeps flowing the right way, and does not simply slosh back and forth with each beat.

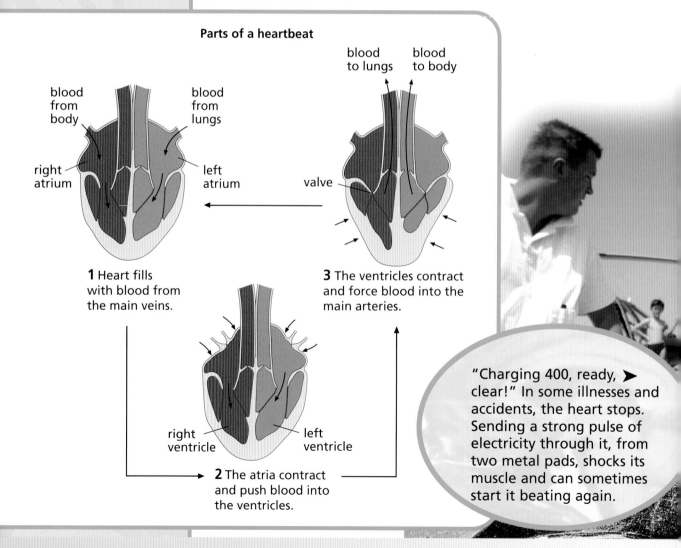

Parts of a heartbeat

blood from body

blood from lungs

right atrium

left atrium

1 Heart fills with blood from the main veins.

blood to lungs

blood to body

valve

3 The ventricles contract and force blood into the main arteries.

right ventricle

left ventricle

2 The atria contract and push blood into the ventricles.

"Charging 400, ready, ➤ clear!" In some illnesses and accidents, the heart stops. Sending a strong pulse of electricity through it, from two metal pads, shocks its muscle and can sometimes start it beating again.

atrium   small, upper pumping chamber of the heart

Upper and lower

Each side of the heart, left and right, has two hollow chambers. The upper one receives blood coming in from the lungs (on the left side) or from the body (on the right side). This chamber, the **atrium,** is small with thin walls. It squeezes weakly to send its blood through a valve into the lower chamber, called the **ventricle.** This has much thicker, more powerful walls. It squeezes strongly to push the blood out through another valve, then around the body (on the left side) or to the lungs (on the right side).

Heartbeats

In general, bigger animals have slower heartbeat rates. But their hearts are much bigger. A whale's heart is the size of a small car!

Beats per minute

Mouse (can you count this fast?)	500
Cat	120
Human	70
Elephant	30
Great whale	10

SPARE PARTS

Sometimes the heart or part of it becomes damaged. Doctors may put in a new part, such as a valve. This is specially made from very tough metal and plastic and should last many years.

ball and cage valve

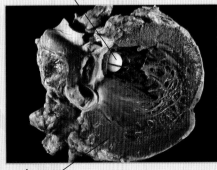

heart

valve   device that controls the flow of a liquid
ventricle   larger, lower pumping chamber of the heart

Hearing the heart

A doctor hears heartbeats through a listening tube called a **stethoscope** (below). The heart's noises can reveal not only its beating rate, but also whether the valves and heart muscle are working properly.

Speed beat

Your heart has one job and that is to pump blood. But this is more complicated than it seems. Sometimes when you are resting or asleep, your muscles and other body parts are not working hard and need little blood. When you play sports or exercise, your muscles do work hard. They need much more blood, maybe five times more, to bring them a lot more **oxygen** and energy. The amazing heart can alter its beating rate and power in a few seconds.

Heart's own muscle

All body parts need blood to bring them oxygen and energy, including the heart with its muscular walls. The blood inside the heart cannot be used for this. It is being squeezed too hard, moving too fast, and in the right side of the heart, it has very little oxygen. So the heart has its own blood tubes, called the **coronary vessels.** They branch over its surface, bringing high oxygen blood for the heart's nonstop work.

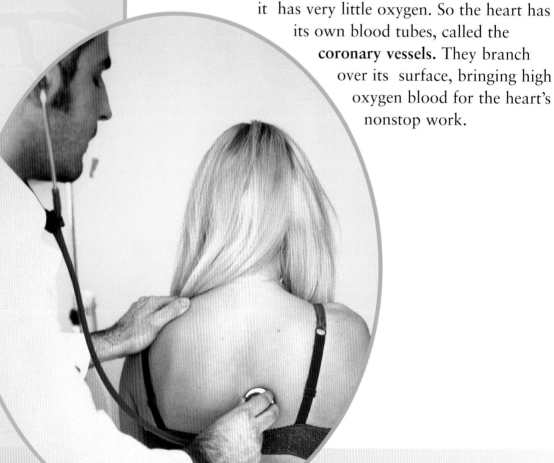

26

coronary vessels arteries and veins that carry blood to and from the heart walls

The body does not have to be very active for its heart to speed up. Feeling scared or frightened can make the heart beat faster and be ready for action in case you need to get away from danger.

Heart attack

In a common form of heart attack, a blood clot blocks a coronary vessel. This usually happens because the vessels have become narrow, stiff, and lumpy inside. This is often partly caused by risky behavior like smoking or eating too much fatty food. The clot, or thrombus, stops blood from reaching the heart muscle, which becomes damaged and cannot pump. This problem is called **coronary thrombosis**.

coronary thrombosis when a lump or clot that blocks a coronary artery to the heart muscle so that it cannot get enough energy or oxygen

Check your own heart rate

As the heart squeezes out blood, its power and pressure make the blood vessels bulge. You can feel this most easily in your wrist. Each heartbeat makes a bulge, called a pulsation. The number of these in one minute is your pulse or heart rate.

Set the pace

Luckily, you don't have to think about how fast or strong your heart is pumping. The automatic part of your brain controls this in two main ways. One way is to send messages to the heart along a **nerve** called the vagus nerve. The other way is to tell body parts called **adrenal glands,** just above the kidneys, to release the substance **epinephrine.** This is a **hormone,** a body control chemical. It travels in the blood to the heart and makes it beat harder and faster.

Pacemakers

When nerve messages and epinephrine reach the heart, they affect a small patch in its upper right side. Doctors call this the sinoatrial node, but most people know it as the pacemaker. It makes sure all the walls of the heart squeeze together at the right time and speed to pump blood smoothly. Occasionally this pacemaker goes wrong. Then doctors can put in an artificial battery-powered pacemaker, to steady and adjust the heartbeat.

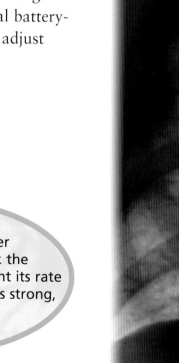

◄ Doctors, nurses, and other medical staff often check the pusle. They not only count its rate but also feel whether it is strong, or weak.

hormones   substances made by hormonal or endocrine glands, which spread around the body in the blood and affect or control the way that various parts work

Heartbeat on screen

When muscles work, they naturally make tiny electrical pulses that pass through the body. The heart muscle's pulses are detected by sensor pads on the skin, and shown as spiky lines on a screen or paper strip. This electrocardiogram, or ECG, tells the doctor about the heart's health.

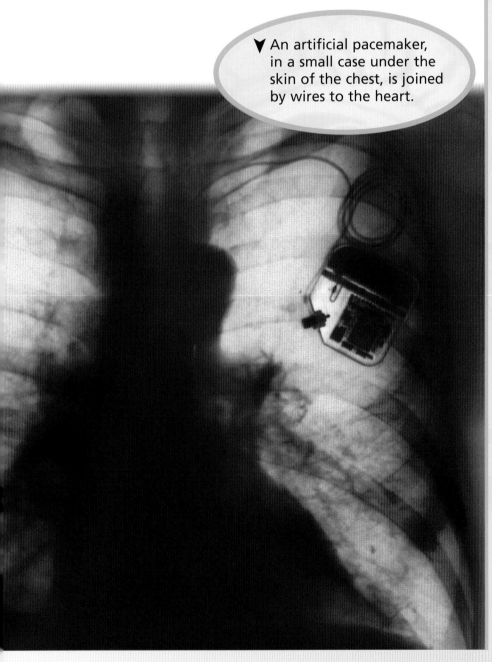

▼ An artificial pacemaker, in a small case under the skin of the chest, is joined by wires to the heart.

Heart facts

At rest
+ Amount of blood pumped with each beat is 0.02 gallon (75 milliliters)
+ Average beating rate is 70 per minute
+ So the heart could fill a bathtub in 23 minutes

During exercise
+ Amount of blood pumped with each beat is over 0.05 gallon (200 milliliters)
+ Average beating rate is 150 per minute
+ So the heart could fill a bathtub in 3 minutes

Number of heartbeats
+ Over 100,000 in one day
+ Almost 40 million in one year
+ Over 3 billion in an average lifetime

nerves stringlike tissues that carry messages around the body as tiny pulses of electricity

Blood Vessels

Every city has a road network of big highways, main streets and smaller roads. These are busy with vans and trucks delivering supplies to factories, schools, and other places. There are also garbage trucks, gathering the waste and trash. Your body's network of blood vessels is like the city's road system. It provides routes all around the body for delivery of oxygen and nutrients and collection of wastes.

Amazing network

The blood system reaches almost every part of the body, from the top of the head to the tips of the fingers and toes. If all your blood vessels could be taken out and joined end to end, they would go twice around the world.

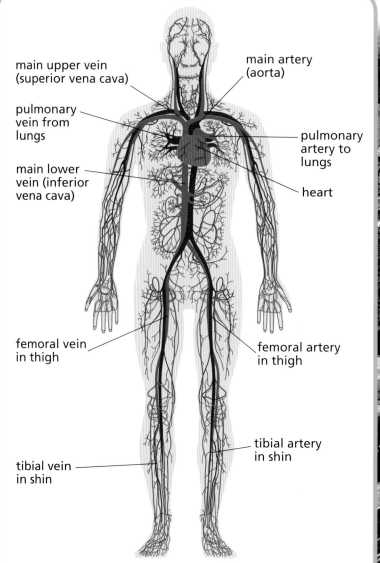

- main upper vein (superior vena cava)
- pulmonary vein from lungs
- main lower vein (inferior vena cava)
- main artery (aorta)
- pulmonary artery to lungs
- heart
- femoral vein in thigh
- femoral artery in thigh
- tibial vein in shin
- tibial artery in shin

arteries　larger blood vessels that carry blood away from the heart
capillaries　tiniest blood vessels with very thin walls

Big, small, big again

There are three main kinds of **blood vessels.** Blood leaving the heart flows through the first kind, **arteries,** which spread out through the body. The arteries divide, becoming smaller and narrower. Finally they form tiny vessels, less than 0.04 inch (1 millimeter) long and far too narrow to see. These are **capillaries,** where blood trades its **oxygen** and nutrients for **carbon dioxide** and wastes. Capillaries gradually join together, becoming bigger and wider. At last they form **veins** that collect blood and take it back to the heart.

Where is my blood?

Veins are much wider than arteries and have thin, stretchy walls. At any single moment, apart from the blood in your heart:
• 14 percent of your blood is in your arteries
• less than 10 percent is in the capillaries
• the rest, about 75 percent, is in your veins.

◄ A road network may look complicated, but the body's blood system is far more complex, and packed into a much smaller place.

vein   large blood vessel that carries blood back to the heart

31

Thick and thin

Artery walls have thick layers of muscles and stretchy fibers to cope with the high pressure surge of blood from each heartbeat. The brain can tell the muscles to contract, which makes the artery narrower. In this way the brain controls blood flow to various body parts.

Highways from the heart

Like the delivery routes around a city, your **arteries** are different sizes. The main **artery** from the heart, the **aorta,** is the major freeway at 16 in (40 cm) long and less than 1 in (25 mm) wide. Blood races along it at 12 in (30 cm) per second, under high pressure. Smaller arteries are about 0.2–0.4 in (5–10 mm) wide. The next smallest arteries, known as **arterioles,** are perhaps just 0.04 in (1 mm) wide.

Less pressure

Arterioles lead to the tiniest blood vessels, **capillaries.** These are like a city's countless small alleys, side streets, and driveways for delivery of goods and collection of wastes.

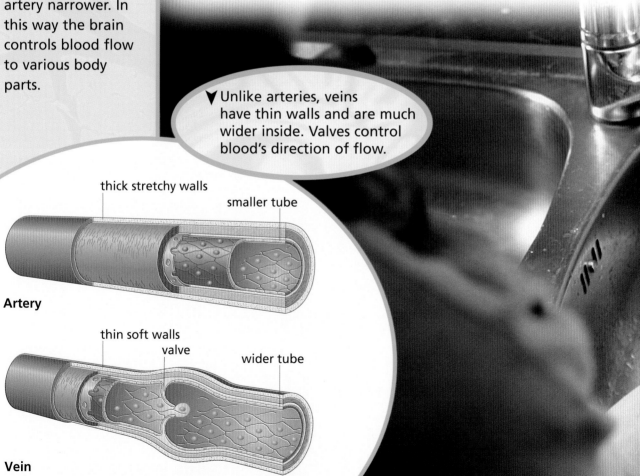

▼ Unlike arteries, veins have thin walls and are much wider inside. Valves control blood's direction of flow.

thick stretchy walls

smaller tube

Artery

thin soft walls

valve

wider tube

Vein

pulmonary artery vessel that takes blood from the heart to the lungs

By the time blood gets to the capillaries it has lost most of its high pressure. It flows on to the smaller **veins,** known as **venules.** These join to form a few very large veins, where blood oozes slowly, under almost no pressure at all. The biggest veins are 16 in (40 cm) long and more than 1.2 in (30 mm) wide.

Walls and valves

Blood flows quicker and under more pressure in arteries. To cope with this pressure, arteries have thick, strong walls. The blood inside veins is under far less pressure, so the walls of veins are thin, stretchy, and soft. Large veins also have valves inside, like those in the heart. These make sure the slow-flowing blood moves the correct way, back to the heart.

Not all red

Arteries carry blood away from the heart, but this blood is not always bright red and high in oxygen. The **pulmonary arteries** to the lungs carry dark reddish-blue, low-oxygen blood. Similarly, the **pulmonary veins** going away from the lungs contain high-oxygen, bright red blood, unlike the rest of the veins, which have dark blood, low in oxygen.

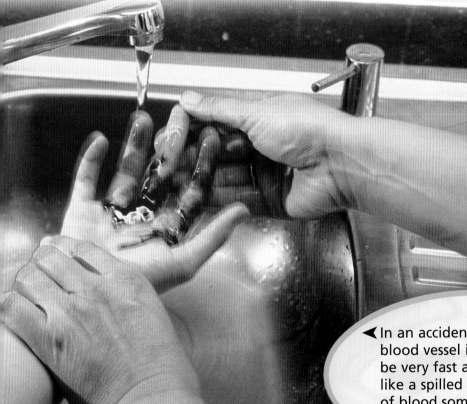

◀ In an accident, when a main blood vessel is cut, blood loss can be very fast and serious. However, like a spilled drink, the amount of blood sometimes looks like more than it is.

One cell thick

The body is made of billions of microscopic building-block **cells,** of many kinds. Capillary walls are just one cell thick. These cells look like paving stones or sidewalk slabs curled around into a tube shape (see below).

Too tiny to see

The body's smallest **blood vessels, capillaries,** are far too tiny to see. But if you could take them all out, make them flat, and join them together into a huge sheet, it would cover about one-fifth of a soccer field. **Oxygen** and nutrients have this huge area to **diffuse** through. Also the sheet would be very thin, just 0.00004 inch (.001 millimeter) making the journey short and easy.

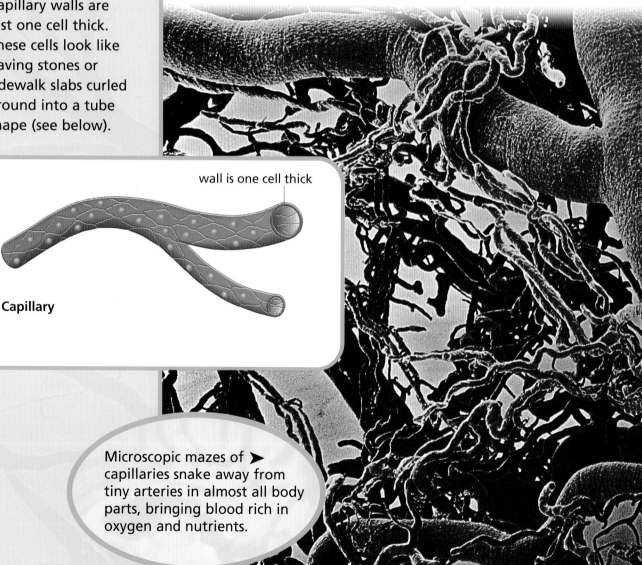

wall is one cell thick

Capillary

Microscopic mazes of ➤ capillaries snake away from tiny arteries in almost all body parts, bringing blood rich in oxygen and nutrients.

lens   part behind the pupil that bends or focuses light towards the inside of the eyeball

Slow blood

Blood flows very slowly through capillaries, only about half a millimeter each second. Since most capillaries are only half a millimeter long, blood takes just one second to pass through. But this is enough time for oxygen and nutrients to pass out of the blood. **Carbon dioxide** and wastes also pass into the blood. This delivery and collection only happens in capillaries. The walls of **arteries** and **veins** are too thick.

DID YOU KNOW?

One of the few places in the body with no capillaries is the lens inside the eye. This must be crystal clear, so we can see through it. Without blood, oxygen and nutrients get into the lens by diffusing in from the parts around.

You look tired

Sometimes people have dark patches like bags or circles under their eyes. When the body is very tired, the heart pumps less quickly, and blood flows slower. It begins to collect in small veins. We see this under the thin skin below each eye as a dark patch.

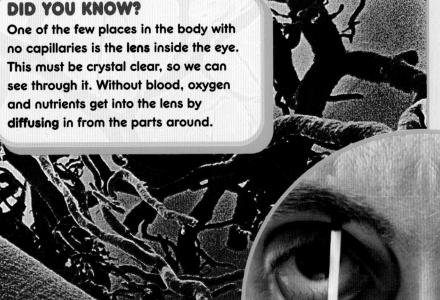

Blood

It is red, thick, sticky and gooey, and never still. Blood is your body's all-purpose liquid, with at least 20 important tasks. It carries **oxygen** to your body's billions of microscopic cells. It also supplies your **cells** with energy in the form of **glucose** (sugar) and with **nutrients** for growth and mending everyday wear-and-tear. Blood collects **carbon dioxide** and wastes from your cells' life processes. It carries body control substances called **hormones**, like the **epinephrine** mentioned earlier. It is the main battleground for your body's fight against germs. And it spreads warmth from busy parts such as hardworking muscles to the rest of the body.

A vampire bat laps up ➤ blood from a big animal like a horse, pig, cow, or human. Since the bat survives on blood alone, blood must contain everything necessary for life. It is complete food.

glucose sugar obtained from the breakdown of other sugars and carbohydrates in food. It is the body's main source of energy.

What is in blood?

Slightly over half of your blood is a pale yellow liquid called **plasma.** This contains most of the nutrients, hormones, and other substances. Slightly less than half of blood is oxygen-carrying **red cells.** About 1/100th of blood is **white cells,** which mainly clean the blood and fight germs and disease. The final 1/100th is tiny parts of cells called **platelets.** These are involved in blood clotting.

HOW MUCH BLOOD?

- Blood makes up about 1/12th of the body's total weight.
- An average large adult has about 1.3 gallons (5 liters) of blood.
- A smaller adult has about 1.1 gallons (4 liters) of blood.

Save a life

Many people can save a life by donating blood from an arm vein. In a few days the body has made enough new blood to replace it. Donated blood is stored at a blood bank. It is **transfused** into people who have lost blood in an accident or during a long operation.

Donated blood is specially treated for storage. It may be split into its various parts such as plasma, red cells, and platelets. A long and complicated operation may use many quarts of blood.

transfusion moving a liquid from one place to another

Color of blood

Blood's color is due to red blood cells. When they have plenty of oxygen from the lungs, they are bright red. When they give up this oxygen and take on carbon dioxide, they become a much darker reddish-blue.

Grab, carry, release

Your blood is red because it contains red blood cells. You have billions and billions of them. Each red blood cell is shaped like a doughnut without the hole. Its special job is to carry **oxygen.** Blood in the lungs needs oxygen but has plenty of **carbon dioxide.** So the red cells take oxygen from the air inside the tiny air bubbles, the **alveoli,** and get rid of carbon dioxide, passing it into the alveoli air bubbles, ready for you to breathe out.

Letting go

Then blood sets off on its journey all around your body. As it flows through the tiny **capillaries,** it passes body cells.

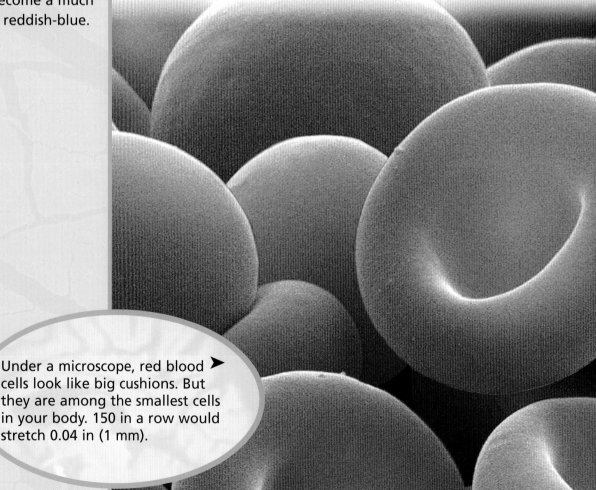

Under a microscope, red blood cells look like big cushions. But they are among the smallest cells in your body. 150 in a row would stretch 0.04 in (1 mm).

iron   metal mineral from food needed by the blood and other parts

If the cells need oxygen, the red blood cells will release their oxygen. They also take away the carbon dioxide that the body cells don't need.

Healthy blood

Red cells contain the mineral **iron.** You need regular supplies of iron in food to keep your blood healthy. People who eat many different foods, especially fresh vegetables and fruits, should get all the iron they need. However some foods with plenty of iron may not be your favorites, such as rhubarb, spinach, and liver.

Look, red cells!

Sometimes we see floaters in our eyes. These tiny circles seem to dart around whenever we try to look straight at them. Often they are red blood cells that have escaped from the eye's blood vessels and are floating in the fluid inside the eye.

What oxygen does

Your lungs breathe, your heart pumps, and your blood flows, all to get **oxygen** to your body's billions of tiny **cells.** But why do they need it? The answer is linked to another important substance that blood delivers to every cell. This is blood sugar, also called **glucose.**

The need for energy

We all need energy to move around, eat, drink, breathe, and simply stay alive. We get this energy from the food we eat. The food is broken into smaller and smaller pieces, including sugars, which contain a lot of energy.

Take-away oxygen

People who go places where there is no oxygen gas, such as scuba divers underwater, must have supplies of oxygen gas to breathe. The carbon dioxide they make has to be breathed out. If its levels rise, it poisons the body.

cellular respiration chemical changes in cells that break apart glucose to release its energy for use by the cells

The sugar travels around your blood stream in the form of glucose **molecules**. Like oxygen, it passes into the body's cells. Inside the cells, this glucose molecule is split apart so the energy in it can be used by your cells to live.

Using oxygen

The cell needs oxygen for the chemical change that will split the glucose molecule and release its energy. As the oxygen is used, carbon dioxide is made. Carbon dioxide is the cell's garbage, and it will be taken away by the red cells in the blood to be breathed out by your lungs. These chemical changes in the cells are called **cellular respiration.**

Making oxygen

People, animals, and plants all need oxygen. So why isn't the oxygen in the air used up? Because fresh supplies are continually made by plants. As plants catch the sun's light energy, they use up carbon dioxide and make oxygen in the process called **photosynthesis**. This is the opposite of respiration. So we must look after our forests, woods, and other plants. We need them!

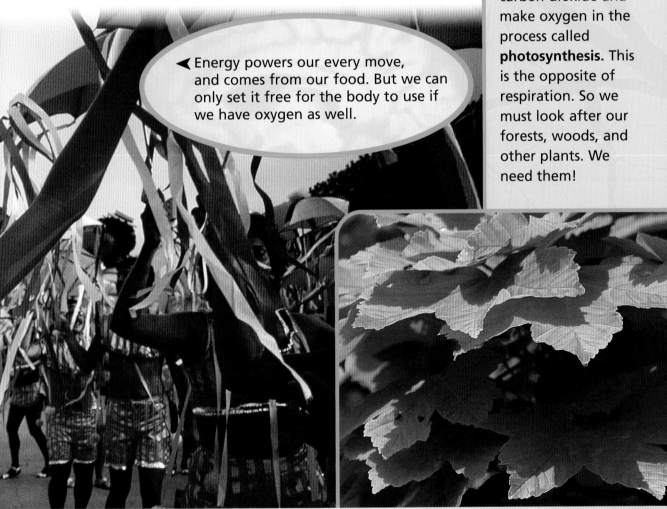

◀ Energy powers our every move, and comes from our food. But we can only set it free for the body to use if we have oxygen as well.

molecule   smallest piece of a substance, such as a nutrient in food

What a clot

When you last had a cut, scrape, or scratch, did it bleed much? Hopefully it stopped quickly because the blood became sticky and lumpy and formed a clot. A clot also stops dirt and germs from getting into your body. When blood leaks and clots beneath your skin, after a hard bump, we call it a bruise.

Lumps, threads, and nets

Clotting starts when tiny pieces in blood called **platelets** become very sticky. They clump together. They also release substances that make tiny strings or threads in the blood, similar to a tangled net.

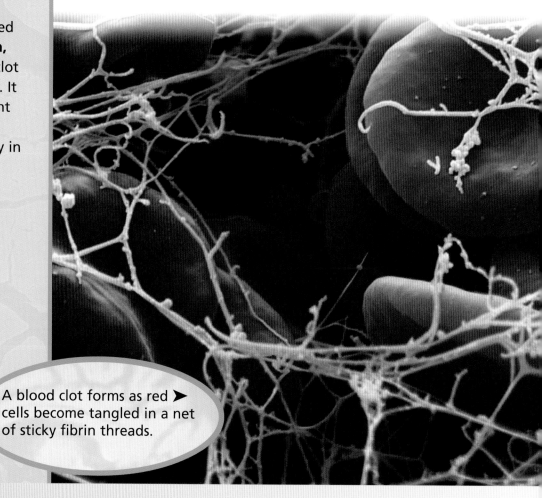

A blood clot forms as red ➤ cells become tangled in a net of sticky fibrin threads.

bone marrow   jellylike substance inside certain bones. It makes new blood cells and stores nutrients.

The net catches more platelets and red blood cells, grows bigger, and becomes a sticky clot. This then becomes hard and dry, forming a scab to protect the area as it heals.

Working together

Clotting is just one of blood's many jobs. But its main task is to be pumped by the heart around the **blood vessels,** carrying **oxygen** that came in through the lungs.

It is an amazing example of how two body systems, respiration and circulation, work closely together. Every second they breathe and pump to keep us alive.

Blood factories

Your blood's red cells, white cells, and platelets (shown magnified below) gradually become damaged and die. Where do you get new ones? These are made in **bone marrow,** the jellylike substance inside your bones. The marrow makes more than two million red cells and two million platelets every second.

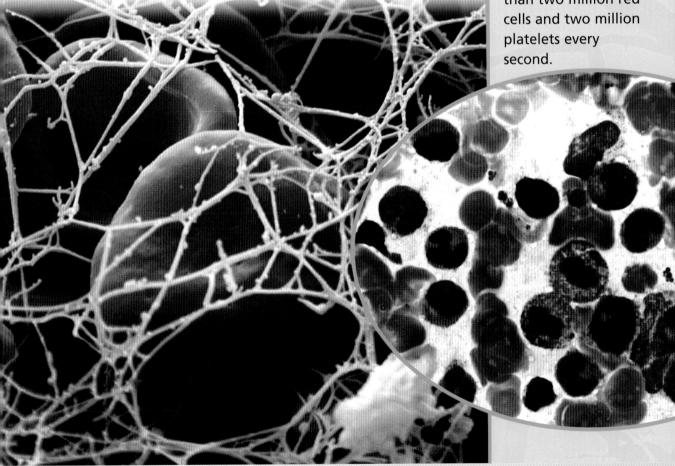

Find Out More

Books

Ballard, Carol. *Heart and Blood*. Chicago: Heinemann Library, 2003

Brynie, Faith Hickman. *101 Questions about Blood and Circulation*. Minneapolis, MN: Lerner Publishing, 2001

Fullick, Ann. *The Human Body*. Chicago: Heinemann Library, 2000

Oleksy, Walter. *The Circulatory System*. New York: Rosen Publishing, 2001

Parker, Steve. *The Heart, Lungs, and Blood*. Chicago: Raintree, 2004

Viegas, Jennifer. *The Heart: Learning How Our Blood Circulates*. New York: Rosen Publishing, 2002

World Wide Web

If you want to find out more about respiration and circulation, you can search the Internet using keywords like these:

- "bronchial tract"
- pace + maker
- respiratory system
- circulation + blood

You can also find your own keywords by using headings or words from this book. Use the search tips on the opposite page to help you find the most useful Web sites.

Where to search 1

Search engine
A search engine looks through millions of Web site pages. It lists all the sites that match the words in the search box. It can give thousands of links, but you will find the best matches are at the top of the list, on the first page. Try **google.com**

Search tips

There are billions of pages on the Internet. It can be difficult to find exactly what you are looking for. These tips will help you find useful Web sites more quickly:

- Know what you want to find out about.
- Use two to six keywords in a search, putting the most important words first.
- Be precise—only use names of people, places, or things.
- If you want to find words that go together, put quote marks around them, for example, "stomach acid" or "length of intestine."
- Use the advanced section of your search engine
- Use the + sign between keywords to link them.

Where to search 2

Search directory

A search directory is like a library of Web sites that have been sorted by a person instead of a computer. You can search by keyword or subject and browse through the different sites like you look through books on a library shelf. A good example is **yahooligans.com**

Glossary

abdomen lower part of the body or torso

adrenal gland gland above the kidney that makes several hormones including epinephrine

allergy the body reacts against a substance that is normally harmless, such as pollen, and fights it as if it is a germ

alveoli tiny bubbles in the lungs, where oxygen is passed into blood vessels and carbon dioxide is taken out

aorta main artery carrying blood away from the left side of the heart

arteries larger blood vessels that carry blood away from the heart

arterioles smaller blood vessels that carry blood away from the heart

asthma condition, often linked to an allergy, in which the bronchioles get narrow and fill with mucus, making breathing difficult

atrium small, upper pumping chamber of the heart

blood vessels arteries, capillaries, and veins through which blood flows

bone marrow jellylike substance inside certain bones. It makes new blood cells and stores nutrients.

bronchi large air tubes that branch from the bottom of the trachea and carry air into the lungs

bronchioles small tubes that take air from the large airways to the deepest parts of the lungs

capillaries tiniest blood vessels with very thin walls

carbon dioxide waste gas made by the body and breathed out

cardiac to do with the heart

cartilage tough, springy substance that forms some parts of the skeleton

cells microscopic building blocks that make up all living things

cellular respiration chemical changes in cells that break apart glucose to release its energy for use by the cells

cilia microscopic hairs on the cells in various body parts, that wave back and forth

clot lump of blood that seals a wound or can block blood flow

contract become smaller or shorter

coronary thrombosis lump or clot that blocks a coronary artery to the heart muscle so that it cannot get enough energy or oxygen

coronary vessels arteries and veins that carry blood to and from the heart walls

diaphragm large sheet of muscle under the lungs

diffusion movement of a substance from a place where there is a lot of it to a place where there is less of it

epinephrine a hormone that gets the body ready for quick action

glottis narrow gap between the vocal cords

glucose sugar obtained from the breakdown of other sugars and carbohydrates in food. It is the body's main source of energy.

hormones substances made by hormonal or endocrine glands, which spread around the body in the blood and affect or control the way that various parts work

intercostals straplike muscles between each pair of ribs

iron metal mineral from food needed by the blood and other body parts

larynx voicebox in the neck

lens part behind the pupil that bends or focuses light towards the inside of the eyeball

molecule smallest piece of a substance, such as a nutrient in food

mucus sticky fluid that helps gather dust and germs and helps substances move easily

myocardium muscle in the walls of the heart

nerves stringlike tissues that carry messages around the body as tiny pulses of electricity

nutrients substances in food that the body needs to grow, be healthy, and heal from injuries

organ major part of the body, such as the brain, liver, or heart

oxygen gas that makes up one-fifth of air, and which the body needs

photosynthesis process in which plants absorb carbon dioxide and light energy to make food and release oxygen

plasma pale yellow liquid part of blood

platelets pieces of cells that are needed in blood clotting

pulmonary artery vessel that takes blood from the heart to the lungs

pulmonary circulation route of blood from the right side of the heart, through the lungs, and back to the left side of the heart

red blood cells cells that carry oxygen around the body

respiratory system nose, mouth, pharynx, larynx, trachea, bronchi, lungs

stethoscope listening device for hearing body sounds

systematic circulation route of blood from the left side of the heart, around the body, and back to the right side of the heart

transfusion moving a liquid from one place to another

valve device that controls the flow of a liquid

vein large blood vessel that carries blood to the heart

ventricle larger, lower pumping chamber of the heart

venules small veins that collect blood from capillaries and join up to form veins

vocal cords two parts on either side of the larynx which vibrate to make the sounds of your voice

white blood cells cells that are specialized to clean the blood and fight germs and diseases

Index